LIVING LARGE

WWE'S SUPERSIZED SUPERSTARS IN ACTUAL SIZE

L. J. TRACOSAS

becker&mayer!
BOOK PRODUCERS

CONTENTS

SUPERSIZED SUPERSTARS

From their towering height to their huge personalities, and from their crazy-strong physiques to their big schemes, WWE Superstars are larger than life! These athletes need to be the biggest and best to dominate their competition in the ring. In these pages, you'll find actual-size photos of the true titans of WWE. Check out how your fist sizes up against Big Show's. How puny does your sneaker look compared to Mark Henry's boot? Do you measure up?

HOW BIG?

Superstars are supersized and super strong, but just how humongous? Here are some comparisons to give you an idea.

- Undertaker is about the size of three 8-year-old boys standing on each other's shoulders.
- Braun Strowman is more than twice as heavy as the average U.S. man.
- Big Show is 7 feet (213 cm) tall. That's about the same height as a male grizzly bear, or just about a foot shorter than an African elephant.
- Mark Henry weighs 399 pounds (181 kg)—as much as a tiger.
- John Cena can lift over 600 pounds (272 kg). That's like lifting an alligator!

4

TRAINING TO BE
TREMENDOUS

Sure, many Superstars are born big and tall, but all of them have training regimens that help them be the best they can be.

John Cena says that you should figure out training that you love to do. Cena loves to lift weights. In fact, when he was 12 years old, he begged his dad for a weight set and has been training ever since. As part of his workout, he does Olympic lifting in quick sets—meaning minimal rest in between each lift. For example, he'll heave 495 pounds (225 kg) in a back squat five times fast.

ALWAYS ATHLETES

Many Superstars started out in different sports before making their way to the WWE. Their size and athleticism made all the difference.

- Roman Reigns played college ball for Georgia Tech and then a bit of pro football in the United States and Canada.
- Mark Henry was an Olympic weightlifter who also crushed all-time world records in squats and deadlifts.

READY TO SEE YOUR FAVORITE WWE SUPERSTARS' STRENGTH IN REAL SIZE? TURN THE PAGE!

JOHN CENA

HUSTLE, LOYALTY, RESPECT

This tough guy from Massachusetts has come a long way. From his first bout with Kurt Angle back in 2002, John Cena has bulldozed through one after another WWE Superstar in the ring— and he has the titles to prove it: 15 World Championships and 5 U.S. Championships. On top of all that, he's a good guy. He truly abides by his "Hustle, Loyalty, Respect" creed. And he's granted more Make-A-Wish requests than any other Superstar.

STATS

HEIGHT 6 feet, 1 inch (185 cm)

WEIGHT 251 pounds (114 kg)

SIGNATURE MOVES
- Attitude Adjustment
- STF

CHAMPIONSHIPS WWE World Heavyweight Champion; World Heavyweight Champion; United States Champion; World Tag Team Champion; WWE Tag Team Champion

RUTHLESS AGGRESSION

You could say that the Cenation was born the day that John Cena's fist connected with Kurt Angle's jaw. From there, the guy just got more intense. The STF is a brutal finishing move. Pinned facedown on the mat, twisted at unnatural angles, and clamped between Cena's beefy forearms? There's no escape.

HEIGHT 6 feet (183 cm)

WEIGHT 212 pounds (96 kg)

SIGNATURE MOVES

- Trouble in Paradise
- Boom Drop
- SOS

CHAMPIONSHIPS

Intercontinental Champion; World Tag Team
Champion; United States Champion; WWE
Tag Team Champion

STATS

KOFI KINGSTON

DYNAMITE DYNAMO

Whether he's flashing a smile or striking a competitor, the Dreadlocked Dynamo is like lightning in the ring. Born in Ghana, Africa, Kofi Kingston moved to the United States, where he became a world-class athlete and found the "power of positivity." And thank goodness! He's a high-flying and high-energy Superstar who electrifies crowds solo or as part of New Day.

CRUSHING KICK

The Dreadlocked Dynamo looks like a human tornado when he launches into the Trouble in Paradise, his signature takedown. WWE Superstars on the receiving end of Kofi's airborne corkscrew kick to the face are left seeing stars.

BRAY WYATT

THE EATER OF WORLDS

Mysterious. Deranged. Nightmare. These are just a few of the words used to describe Bray Wyatt. Compelled by forces outside of this realm, and spurred on by the energy of his flock, Wyatt is a dangerous force to be reckoned with. Where he comes from, everything burns.

LOOK AT THAT FACE

Here it is: the New Face of Fear. Backed by the Wyatt Family, Bray Wyatt is bringing his dark message to the masses. No one knows where his mission will lead him next. Whether he's calling out Undertaker or being forced to team up with Roman Reigns, Wyatt's always with the buzzards–and following his calling.

STATS

HEIGHT 6 feet, 3 inches (190 cm)

WEIGHT 285 pounds (129 kg)

SIGNATURE MOVES

- Sister Abigail

STATS

6 feet (183 cm)

218 pounds (99 kg)

• Zig Zag

World Heavyweight Champion;
Intercontinental Champion; United
States Champion, Money in the Bank
Ladder Match winner

DOLPH ZIGGLER

A SUPERSTAR AMONG SUPERSTARS

There's no doubt about it: Dolph Ziggler has it all: the looks, the moves, *and* a good sense of humor. Ziggler wows nearly every time he's in the ring—a trend he started setting in college, where he pinned his way to the top of the amateur wrestling scene. He continued his championship streak when he joined WWE, winning World Heavyweight, Intercontinental, and United States Championships. This wonder of the ring proves he's the best in the business again and again.

CORE STRENGTH

With the Zig Zag, Dolph Ziggler sends his target straight to the mat with a punishing pounding. To achieve this, WWE's pretty boy needs some serious core strength to launch, grab, and slam, laying any Superstar who crosses him down flat.

15

BRAUN STROWMAN

7'

6'

5'

4'

3'

2'

1'

THE NEW FACE OF DESTRUCTION

Braun Strowman is a mad mountain of man and muscle, and he adds some serious strength to the New Force of Destruction that is the Wyatt Family. His giant arms are like cement clotheslines–just ask Roman Reigns, who was out cold after colliding with one.

HEIGHT:
6 feet, 8 inches (182 cm)
WEIGHT:
395 pounds (179 kg)

STATS

ABIGAIL'S BLACK SHEEP

Nearly 7 feet (213 cm) tall and unbelievably broad, Braun Strowman looms large in the Wyatt Family flock. He has a wild stare and a supernatural strength, and he seems propelled by a power outside of himself. There's no doubt that the Eater of Worlds hand-picked Braun for punishing purposes.

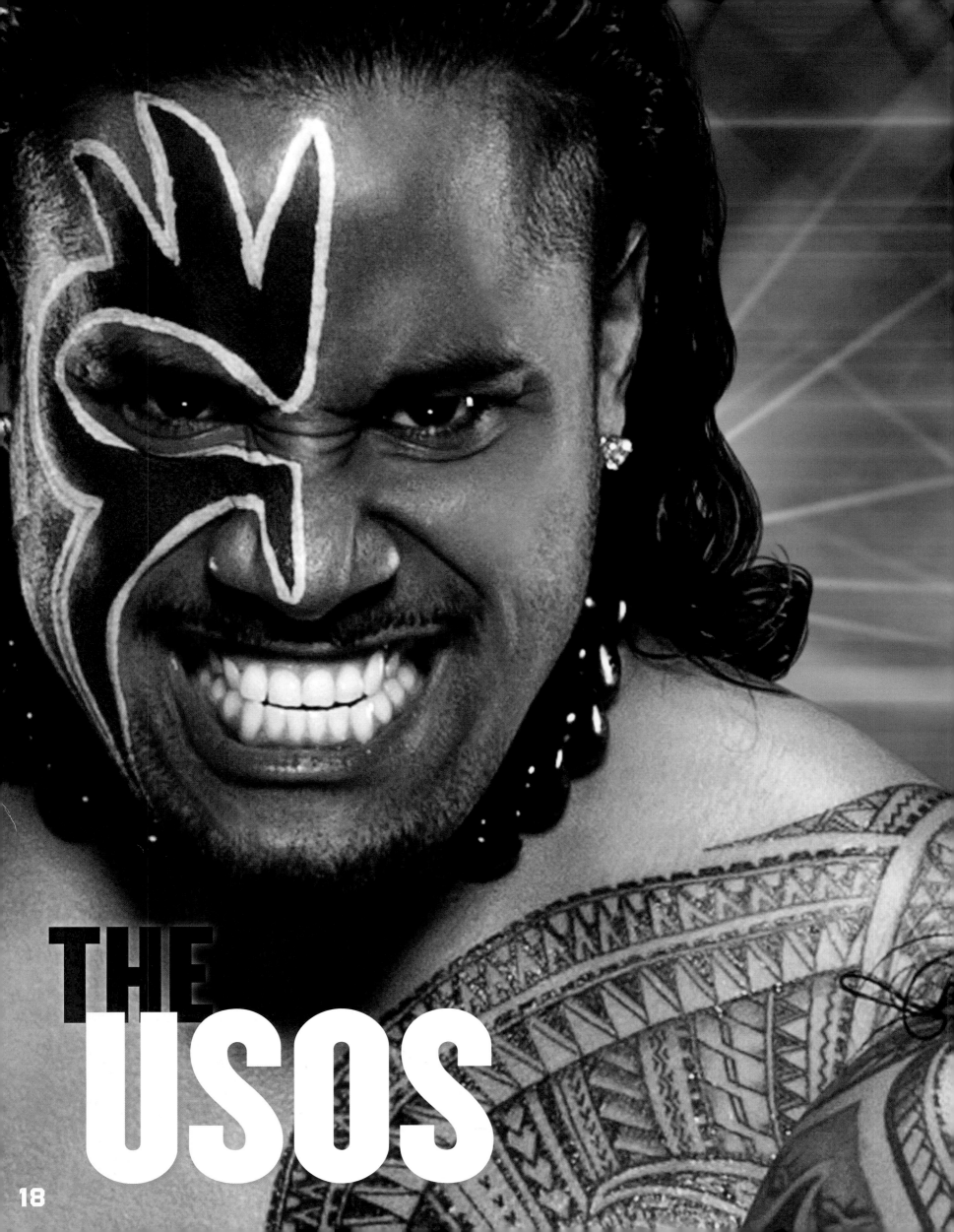

THE USOS

MODERN WARRIORS

As members of the legendary Samoan Anoa'i Family, The Usos come from a tradition of greatness. They channel their ancestors before every match in the Siva Tau, an old Samoan war dance designed to terrify. But outside of that, there's nothing traditional about The Usos. They electrify the ring with their energy and bold looks, from their face paint to their boots.

DOUBLE WHAMMY

The Usos are synched up in a way other tag teams aren't. This high-energy and high-flying pair are twins, and they come from a long line of Samoan Superstars. From their Double Superkicks to the Double Samoan Splash, Jimmy and Jey smack down in stereo.

JIMMY

HEIGHT: 6 feet, 3 inches (190 cm)

WEIGHT: 251 pounds (114 kg)

JEY

HEIGHT: 6 feet, 2 inches (188 cm)

WEIGHT: 228 pounds (103 kg)

STATS

SIGNATURE MOVES:
- Alley-UCE
- Double Samoan Splash
- Double Superkick

CHAMPIONSHIPS: WWE Tag Team Champions

7'

6'

5'

4'

3'

2'

1'

UNDERTAKER

THE LAST OUTLAW

When the bell tolls, Superstars everywhere feel the chill of sports entertainment's Grim Reaper. Undertaker has been a supernatural force in WWE for more than 25 years, burying foes and tearing down champions with Tombstones and Chokeslams. It doesn't matter who you are; the Deadman is coming for you.

HE WON'T REST IN PEACE

Undertaker blazed a legendary trail in WWE with hellfire. One of the Phenom's truly otherworldly accomplishments? The Streak: his 21-0 winning record at *WrestleMania*. The Deadman managed to bury the competition for years, until Brock Lesnar bested him at *WrestleMania 30*. Even though Undertaker resurrected his winning ways the next year, you know he won't forget that defeat anytime soon.

STATS

6 feet, 10 inches (208 cm)

299 pounds (136 kg)

- Chokeslam
- Tombstone
- Last Ride

WWE Champion; World Heavyweight Champion; World Tag Team Champion; WCW Tag Team Champion; Hardcore Champion

SUPERSIZED SUPERSTARS & LARGER-THAN-LIFE LEGENDS

The current WWE Superstars are some of the most massive and muscular athletes in all of sports and entertainment, but the WWE Universe has always been stocked with impressive Superstar specimens. Take a look at today's Superstars standing toe-to-toe with Superstars of the past.

ENORMOUS GIANTS

Big Show towers over other Superstars in the ring these days, but Andre the Giant's legacy casts a long shadow in terms of supersized Superstars. Born in a small village in France, Andre was growing to epic proportions from an early age: When he was 12 years old, he was as tall as Triple H and weighed more than Kalisto. Andre was a true Superstar and was undefeated in WWE for 15 years. Bow down to the Giant!

7 feet, 4 inches (223 cm)
520 pounds (235 kg)

7 feet (213 cm)
450 pounds (204 kg)

CREEPY COLLOSUS

Bray Wyatt sends shivers down the collective spine of the WWE Universe today. But Kane terrified Superstars and fans alike when he set WWE ablaze in the early 2000s. Propelled toward destruction by a dark flame burning within, Kane kidnapped Superstars and lit up WWE Hall of Famers (literally).

7 feet (213cm)

323 pounds (146 kg)

6 feet, 3 inches (190 cm)

285 pounds (129 kg)

BIG BAD BOYS

As gargantuan as these guys are, their rivalry was bigger. The Rock and Stone Cold dominated the Attitude Era of WWE in the late 1990s. Though Stone Cold retired from WWE after *WrestleMania XIX*, his legendary rivalry with the People's Champion still resonates today.

6 feet, 5 inches (196 cm)

260 pounds (118 kg)

6 feet, 2 inches (187 cm)

252 pounds (114 kg)

BIG SHOW

JUST GINORMOUS

Man or mammoth? Big Show is easily one of WWE's most supersized Superstars. At 7 feet (213 cm) tall and more than 400 pounds (181 kg), it's clear he's the World's Biggest Athlete. From the moment he steps into a match—by simply stepping over the top rope—Big Show's a colossal threat.

STATS

7 feet (213 cm)

450 pounds (204 kg)

- KO Punch
- Chokeslam
- Colossal Clutch

CHAMPIONSHIPS WWE Champion; World Heavyweight Champion; ECW World Champion; WCW Champion; World Tag Team Champion; WWE Hardcore Champion; United States Champion; WWE Tag Team Champion; Intercontinental Champion; 2015 Andre the Giant Memorial Battle Royal winner

SHOW'S SHOWDOWN

With his massive measurements, Big Show's fist is a battering ram. His KO Punch means lights out for anyone it meets. After being fired by Stephanie McMahon in 2013, Show returned to the ring and fired up the crowd. He tossed the Shield aside like ragdolls and delivered a booming knockout blow to Chief Operating Officer Triple H.

ROMAN REIGNS

A TOTAL POWERHOUSE

Is Roman Reigns a sinister slayer or proud warrior? Whether part of the Shield or on his own, this former footballer dives headfirst into battle–both in attitude and using the Spear, the piercing move that he's perfected. Reigns intends to roll over any Superstar between him and a win.

STATS

6 feet, 3 inches (190 cm)

265 pounds (120 kg)

- Spear
- Superman Punch

WWE World Heavyweight Champion; WWE Tag Team Champion; 2015 Royal Rumble Match winner; 2014 Superstar of the Year Slammy Award winner

SUPERMAN PUNCH

Packed with power, the Superman Punch is high-flying and full of force. It's a fast-moving fist with the full weight of Reigns behind it. The Superman Punch has collided with Superstars from John Cena to Sheamus—and it has cleared the path all the way to the WWE World Heavyweight Championship.

BROCK LESNAR

7'
6'
5'
4'
3'
2'
1'

AN ABLE ANIMAL

Brock Lesnar is a savage in the ring. The Beast Incarnate is an intense fighter, and he draws on his success as a college wrestler, his skill in mixed martial arts, as well as his animal strength to crush competitors. Lesnar is ready to show any competitor who crosses him the way to Suplex City.

STATS

HEIGHT: 6 feet, 3 inches (191 cm)

WEIGHT: 286 pounds (130 kg)

SIGNATURE MOVES:
- F-5
- Kimura Lock

CHAMPIONSHIPS: WWE World Heavyweight Champion; 2002 King of the Ring; 2003 Royal Rumble Match winner

SUPERSONIC STRENGTH

The Beast Incarnate's physique is serious stuff. He's got muscles built for mangling, which he does easily by applying the Kimura Lock. Most impressive, though, is a win he'll be remembered for forever: Using three devastating F-5s, he drained Undertaker of his supernatural strength to end the Deadman's 21-straight *WrestleMania* winning streak.

SHEAMUS

WORLDWIDE WARRIOR

Sheamus doesn't need the luck of the Irish. This Dubliner is a brawler who's ready for a fight. Those bouts don't always last long, though. With a lightning-quick Brogue Kick to the face, Sheamus knocked out Daniel Bryan in 18 seconds at *WrestleMania XXVIII*. The first Irish-born WWE Superstar, Sheamus formed the League of Nations with Superstars hailing from other countries—and it's now an international force to reckoned with.

"I'M BACK"

After resting an injury, Sheamus sped back into the ring in 2015, chasing away Bad News Barrett and clobbering his former friends Daniel Bryan and Dolph Ziggler. The bad attitude was a surprise, but so was the Great White's new look: He rocked a fiery mohawk and beard braids.

STATS

HEIGHT: 6 feet, 4 inches (193 cm)

WEIGHT: 267 pounds (121 kg)

SIGNATURE MOVES:
- Brogue Kick
- Celtic Cross
- White Noise

CHAMPIONSHIPS: WWE Champion; United States Champion; 2010 King of the Ring; 2012 Royal Rumble Match winner; World Heavyweight Champion; 2015 Money in the Bank Contract winner

MARK HENRY

An Olympian, a Pan American weightlifting medalist, and winner of the World's Strongest Man competition in 2002: Mark Henry has earned his nickname, "The World's Strongest Man," by lifting barbells *and* some of the biggest Superstars in his 20 years in WWE. Just ask anyone on the receiving end of the World's Strongest Slam.

STATS

HEIGHT: 6 feet, 4 inches (195 cm)

WEIGHT: 399 pounds (180 kg)

SIGNATURE MOVE:
- World's Strongest Slam

CHAMPIONSHIPS: World Heavyweight Champion; ECW Champion; European Champion

7'
6'
5'
4'
3'
2'
1'

CRUSHING THE COMPETITION

Weighing in at nearly 400 pounds (181 kg), Mark Henry is one of the biggest WWE Superstars *ever*. He's a wall in the ring. When a competitor bounces off the turnbuckle and runs smack into his size 16EEE boot, they have definitely entered the Hall of Pain.

THE MIZ

BECAUSE HE'S THE MIZ . . .

Say what you will about Miz, but you have to acknowledge this Superstar has an eye for opportunity. After all, his in-ring career catapulted into the spotlight when he decided to cash in on his Money in the Bank win to take down an already roughed-up Randy Orton for the WWE World Heavyweight Championship. Why? Because he's The Miz.

. . . AND HE'S AWESOME

Sure, he's got an ego the size of his pecs and a bad attitude to match, but Miz has a pretty face. In fact, it's his moneymaker, whether it's featured on reality TV, The Miz TV, or movies. His mug will get him far, as long as he can keep it from getting bashed in—which he definitely didn't manage to do when A.J. Styles knocked out his tooth veneers during a match in February 2016.

STATS

HEIGHT 6 feet, 2 inches (188 cm)

WEIGHT 221 pounds (100 kg)

SIGNATURE MOVES
- Skull-Crushing Finale
- Figure-Four Leglock

CHAMPIONSHIPS WWE Champion; Intercontinental Champion; United States Champion; WWE Tag Team Champion; World Tag Team Champion; Unified Tag Team Champion; Money in the Bank Ladder Match winner

KALISTO

FLYING FIGHTER

Nicknamed the King of Flight for good reason, Kalisto practically winged into the ring. He competed his way through bouts in Mexico as a *luchador* before pinning his sights on WWE. Teamed up with Sin Cara, Kalisto is one half of the Lucha Dragons. On his own, he's a soaring Superstar who's capable of big wins.

STATS

HEIGHT: 5 feet, 6 inches (168 cm)

WEIGHT: 170 pounds (77 kg)

SIGNATURE MOVE:
- Salida del Sol

CHAMPIONSHIPS: United States Champion; 2015 'OMG!' Shocking Moment of the Year Slammy Award winner

MASKED MAN

Born in Chicago, Kalisto moved to Mexico City, where he got his start as a *luchador*, or a masked Superstar. The vibrant, multicolor masks can hide his face, but they can't hide his talent. This acrobatic wrestler takes flight off of the ropes and seems to hang in the air before bringing the pain down on his foes.

THE ROCK

JUST BRING IT!

Dwayne "The Rock" Johnson is a high-caliber Superstar. Since he first burst into WWE ring in 1996, he's been electrifying fans with his amazing mix of athletics and attitude. With a personality as big as his bicep, the People's Champ is ready to smack down any competition.

STATS

HEIGHT 6 feet, 5 inches (196 cm)

WEIGHT 260 pounds (118 kg)

SIGNATURE MOVES
- Rock Bottom
- People's Elbow

CHAMPIONSHIPS WWE Champion; Intercontinental Champion; World Tag Team Champion; 2000 Royal Rumble match winner; WCW Champion

7'
6'
5'
4'
3'
2'
1'

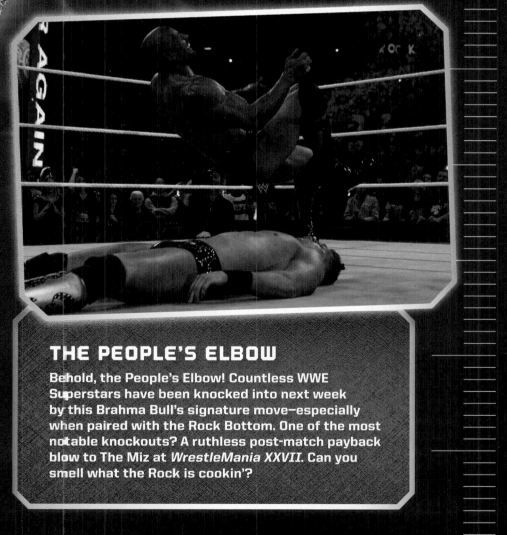

THE PEOPLE'S ELBOW

Behold, the People's Elbow! Countless WWE Superstars have been knocked into next week by this Brahma Bull's signature move—especially when paired with the Rock Bottom. One of the most notable knockouts? A ruthless post-match payback blow to The Miz at *WrestleMania XXVII*. Can you smell what the Rock is cookin'?

This edition published by Scholastic Inc., 557 Broadway, New York, NY 10012, by arrangement with becker&mayer! LLC. Scholastic and associated logos are trademarks and/or registered trademarks of Scholastic Inc.

Scholastic Inc., New York, NY

becker&mayer!
BOOK PRODUCERS

WWE Living Large is produced by becker&mayer!
11120 NE 33rd Place, Suite 101
Bellevue, WA 98004
www.beckermayer.com

Author: L. J. Tracosas
Designers: Rosanna Brockley & Megan Sugiyama
Editor: Dana Youlin
Production coordinator: Tom Miller

Printed in China
10 9 8 7 6 5 4 3 2 1
ISBN: 978-1-60380-394-6
16219